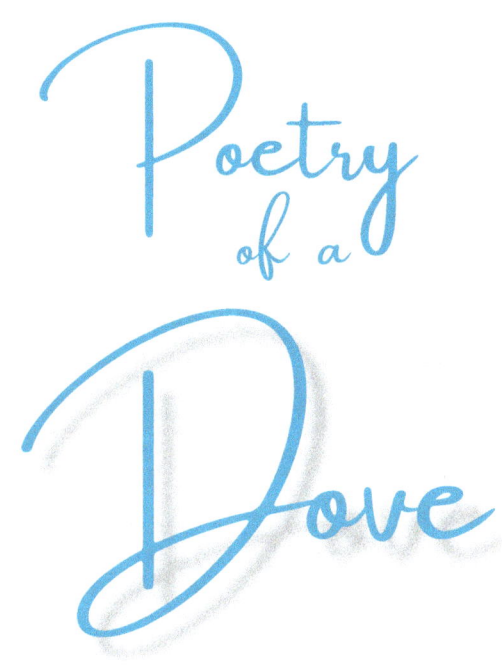

Poetry of a Dove

Michelle Lee Carter

ISBN 978-0-6485028-1-4
© Michelle Lee Carter, 2019

Published by Africa World Books Pty. Ltd.
(www.africaworldbooks.com)

All rights reserved. No part of this publication may be reproduced, stored in a retrieval system, or transmitted, in any form, or by any means, electronic, mechanical, photo-copying, recording or otherwise, without the prior permission of the publishers.

This book is sold subject to the conditions that it shall not, by way of trade or otherwise, be lent, re-sold, hired out or otherwise circulated without the publisher's prior consent in any form of binding or cover other than in which it is published and without a similar condition including the condition being imposed on the subsequent purchaser.

Design and typesetting: All In One Book Design
(www.allinonebookdesign.com.au)

I was brought up in a foster home, when I was 9-years-old a Sunday school teacher came to our school and told us about Jesus. I was instantly attracted to His name and the Sunday school teacher said "Give all of your heart". So I went to my Nanna's that weekend and got on my knees and gave Jesus my heart.

All turned to doom when I was abused by a step-dad, it crushed my faith and belief about myself.

I grew to lead a sinful life and left home when I was 18-years-old. But something was tugging at me to know Jesus again, it was a beautiful, still voice.

When I turned 29 I was sick of my sinful life and decided to join a church but I still struggled. I spent about 18 years in and out of mental hospitals but was still believing for a miracle.

Finally my hospital stays ended as I drew closer to Jesus. Then I was diagnosed with breast cancer having two lumps. So I sat and read God's word over it and not long after this the Holy Spirit intervened and said your breast cancer is healed! Sure enough the biopsy was clear no more cancer!

I have a very supportive husband and family who have seen me through my illness and been there for me.

I decided I would put some uplifting poetry in a book with part proceeds going to the needy.

I now live for Jesus and have much to thank Him for. MY life is now Christ's and I long to see others saved and to see the poor free and abused saved and to come to Christ.

Michelle Lee Carter

This is a collection of poems written in hope you enjoy and take heed because:

Jesus is the way and the truth and the life
John 4-16

God bless
Michelle Lee Carter

Contents

Jesus Said	7
Worship	8
The Blessed Tree	9
To My People	10
Where Is My Help	11
His Precious Tears	12
Little Bird	13
Most High God	14
Jesus Will Come	15
Sweet Surrender	16
The World	17
On This Day	18
Jesus Is Higher	19
Jesus Is Coming Back	20
Come	21
Heaven's Door	22
Praise Your Name	23
Mansion	24
The Light	25
Silent Love	26
Blue Rose	27
The Son	28
Mighty Jesus	29
The Lamb Of God	30
The Horse	31
Angels On High	32

Jesus said...

Jesus said I am the way the truth and the life
I come with my sword and majesty on high
I am the rock your salvation I died for a price
Victory is mine, its yours I gave you my life.

Who comes to help you from the heavens above
To help you in trouble to help you overcome

I am the door I let my sheep in
I died for all humankind I died for all sins

I ride upon the clouds I'm strong gentle and kind
I came to save the sick the poor and the blind

When you call out to Me I will show you my arms out wide
The cross I died upon my hands and feet for all humankind

I rose and went to hell for three days and nights
For you my disciples I won't give up the good fight
So when you feel broken just call out to Me
I am the way the truth the life and the only way you'll be truly free

Worship

The humble Jesus born on Christmas day
In a manger He did lay
To bring good news to the Earth
The noble man of sandalwood silver and mirth
The star in the sky shone so bright
Here is born the true light

Come now worship this child this night
The Earth rejoice the holy birth in sight

Jesus Saviour born for us
To preach the good news without any lust

Thank you Jesus for this given day
And to seek you and humbly pray

The Blessed Tree

The blessed tree you died upon
The sin you took that is my song
Your blessed light no evil can stand
You've blessed ourselves our toil our land

Your my song i sing each day and night
Your heavens darling my complete light

I put my armour on each day
No more evil it's to go away
I pray your touch for my loved ones
How lovely to know the Son

You are the only way and the best
OH how lovely He gave me rest
So I sing a new song
God is my refuge and for everyone

To My People

To the one who comes to me I will no means cast out
I am the way the truth so dance and shout
If you are thirsty come to Me
I will fill your thirst and give you victory

How precious are the feet
To bring good news and the truly meek

The true light the only true way
Will abide in you fully when you pray

When all seems lost and you are in pain
Call to me with all your heart don't come in vain

My thoughts are higher than yours and my ways
So listen to Me dear child to what I say

Where is My Help?

Where is my help it does come
From Jesus in the heavens above

Who is my song that I sing each morn
It is Jesus who died with a crown of thorns

My Saviour whom I adore and love more each day
He will save me from all dismay

And in the night I'll sing His song
Jesus Christ the mighty one so won't you come along?

I do thank you for reading this far again
Now you know He won't be long so don't come in vain

His Precious Tears

Tears are collected for My people I asked
Then poured in a sea of glass

Jesus tears fell rolling down His cheek
Into the abyss where the wretched have no sleep...

Jesus wept
John 11-35

Little Bird

Little bird in the sky
How I love to watch you fly
When your precious feet land to the ground
What a lovely chirp you sound

When you come back again
I will say you're my friend
So little bird I will say
You will come back my way

So this time on earth I've had with you
How I wish to be there too
So little bird in the sky
I with you will never die

Most High God

Most high God Your angels on high
draw me closer draw me nigh

God of Isaac my dream fulfilled
To sing for you is such a thrill

God of Abraham I love to write
About you day and night

God of Jacob we lift your name
That we will never be the same!

Jesus Will Come

Justice will come like the sweet rain
Because no child should stay in pain

Because God helps the hurtful soul
Justice He brings and self control

So i sing a new love song
All God's children do belong

And in the morning and in the night
We are precious in His sight

So play the lute and the harp
Sing His song and laugh

Dance sing and shout a praise
For justice has come and love stays

Sweet Surrender

Yes, I have written there is only one way
To the Father in heaven Jesus Spirit reins

Sweet surrender I surrender all
The evil one rebuked and under our feet we stand tall

So i pray to Jesus each day
I humbly welcome Him on my knees to pray

Jesus is so pure and you can't get Him out of your mind
For He says who He says He is and most holy and kind...

The World

To be adored by the world could lead you away
From the most precious thing not of the world today

The light of the world who's Jesus Christ
Died for you at a precious price

This world will fade away soon
Behold He comes in the clouds for you!

On This Day

On this day of love
Peace came as a dove
The rain gently fell
The good news we did tell
At last there was freedom everywhere
To the King Jesus we gave all our cares
The sun seemed brighter the moon blood red
Did this mean Jesus was coming as it is said
All the Saints were ready to meet Him in the clouds so high
Changed like a twinkle in the eye
Every girl and guy
They were the ones saved they had reached for Him each night and day
Every tear wiped forever was a brand new forever day!

Jesus Is Higher

Jesus is higher than the angels now
We looked to the heavens and knew just how

And Jesus sits upon the throne
So you can pray and never be alone

And great is His love and so high
When you're in need look to Him in the sky

We are protected by His staff and rod
Consider, consider there is no loss

Jesus Is Coming Back

Jesus is coming back my way
With a thousand angels I pray
Jesus is coming back on a white horse
Come now hear His still sweet voice
He is coming back with great glory and power
He said you don't know the hour

Jesus is coming for His true people soon
Behold He comes in the clouds for you
Jesus coming back my way
Nothing can stop His coming this is true I say

Jesus is coming for the poor and the meek
Will you as it is said be asleep?

Jesus is coming back on a white horse
So dear people lift up your voice
The sick the humble He is coming for you
With great glory this is true

Come

I am your Lord God in the sky
Worship Me
I dry your tears from your eyes
The thunder may crash
The lightening fall
Stand close to Me child
And you will stand tall
My angels will guard you
In everything you do
Look up to the heavens
For God loves you!

Heaven's Door

Believe in Jesus all of the time
That is why I write this rhyme
Jesus has glory and is deep within
Believe in Him He will let you in
Otherwise hell could be your dark fate
You'll get to heaven's door and the angels will cry "too late"

So what for you is it going to be?
With Jesus in heaven eternally?
Because it is your choice and God is in control
Yes believe in Him then you're on your way home
Yes believe, receive and repent
God will then never resent
Because He sent His only Son to die on the cross
Consider, consider there is no loss!

Praise Your Name

Praise your name Lord Jesus
Want to lift it on high for the world to see
You're our King Lord Jesus forever more for eternity I give my love to you
My Lord my king my saviour my lover true
And if I fell in love it'd be only you

With your strength and power I will never be the same again
I give my love to you

Your angels are a heavenly grace and forever more
I give my love to you

Mansion

I write a rhyme I write is true
Is there room for you?
Is there a mansion in the perfect sky?
Will you be there is that where you will reside?

Is there an angel showing you the way?
Did God send him or a thousand I pray?

Will we meet in the heavens I say?
Will we be united this I've sometimes prayed

We live together or will we die?
I hope we make it to the mansion in the sky!

Let not your heart be troubled,
ye believe in God, believe also in Me.

In my Father's house are many
mansions, if it were not so I would
have told you.

I go to prepare a place for you.

John 14-1-2

The Light

When tomorrow comes
You may find the light
When everything seems gone
You may find the light

Silent Love

His silent breath
Jesus so broken
He was broken for you
He was broken for me
His gentle ways
He welcomes you
And covers our sin
I love and cherish you
Out of the world
I chose you
Blood on the wooden cross
So clear and true
With arms wide open
I died for you

Blue Rose

Beautiful boy blue rain
We looked to the heavens
To know you weren't in pain
A sweet blue rose over you
We're sharing your love
That's coming through
Take your hurts
And bury them deep
Hold my hand
I shall not weep
Upon a star that burns bright
Blue rose into the light
Of all the loves that I have met
You're the one I won't forget
I'll give the angels back their wings
And risk the loss of everything
Take your hurts
And bury them deep
Hold my hand I shall not weep
Upon a star that burns bright
Blue rose into the light
Sweet girl I give you your dreams
I also know where you have been
When you feel lost call out to me
I will surly set you free
Take your hurts and bury them deep
Hold my hand I shall not weep
Upon a star that burns bright
Blue rose into the light
Sweet blue rose I know your pain
Sweet blue rose blue rain…

The Son on Christmas morn
The Son the crown of thorns

He will bring us light
He is my forever plight

How lovely to set us free
With His Spirit He does lead

I honour Jesus for what He has done
In Christ there is victory for everyone

Worship the King of Kings this Christmas time
Oh hall Ilya the Son is mine

Thank you Jesus for your given grace
Oh how lovely to seek your face

Mighty Jesus

Jesus mighty angels on high
Draw me closer draw me nigh
Help me to win the race
As it is your goodness that I taste

The dead are raised the sick are healed
In God almighty this road is real

So awaken you people who sleep
Welcome the stranger and the widow who weeps
Help the meek and the poor
Feed them food and Christ who is adored

Give thanks to the only one
For in Christ you have won!

The Lamb of God

The king of kings and lamb of God
I'm in your heart I'm in your strode
I'm patient loving and kind
I came to save the captive the poor and the blind
I wait for you to ask Me in
I'm the only one who can forgive your sin
I'll help you just call to Me
I'll forgive your sin and set you free

The Horse

The horse and Jesus become upon the clouds
To judge the people here and now

The mighty Saviour has come to judge all
For good and bad with some may fall

And so we say my weary friends
Could this be the very end?

So here we are my tall friends
May you be righteous till the end!

Angels On High

The mighty angels lift Jesus name
Helping the poor and the lame

"He is exalted on high"
"Come draw closer come draw nigh"

The angels are holy they help in time of need
"Jesus is mighty" now you have sewn the seed

Gracious abounding is Jesus love
"Come fill us dear Jesus it's more than enough"

So now we get closer to the clouds above
"He has come now closer" and the holy dove

The angels cry out "He is coming soon"
Behold cry out for He is coming to you!

www.ingramcontent.com/pod-product-compliance
Lightning Source LLC
Chambersburg PA
CBHW052309300426
44110CB00035B/2313